TRANSPORTATION ADVENTURES

Written by Doug Barone

UNDER THE GROUND

KidHaven PUBLISHING

Published in 2027 by
KidHaven Publishing, an Imprint of Greenhaven Publishing, LLC
2544 Clinton St., Buffalo, NY 14224

Written by: Doug Barone
Edited by: Rebecca Phillips-Bartlett
Designed by: Ker Ker Lee

Cataloging-in-Publication Data

Names: Barone, Doug.
Title: Under the ground / Doug Barone.
Description: Buffalo, NY : KidHaven Publishing, 2027. | Series: Transportation adventures | Includes glossary and index.
Identifiers: ISBN 9781534569775 (pbk.) | ISBN 9781534569782 (library bound) | ISBN 9781534569799 (ebook)
Subjects: LCSH: Tunnels--Transportation--Juvenile literature. | Subways--Juvenile literature. | Underground construction--Juvenile literature. | Transportation--Juvenile literature.
Classification: LCC TA807.B376 2027 | DDC 388.42--dc23

Printed in China

CPSIA compliance information: Batch #QS27KH: For further information contact Greenhaven Publishing LLC at 1-844-317-7404.

Please visit our website, www.greenhavenpublishing.com.
For a free color catalog of all our high-quality books, call toll free 1-844-317-7404 or fax 1-844-317-7405.

Find us on

Photo Credits – Images courtesy of Shutterstock.com, unless otherwise stated.

Cover & Recurring – muratart, J Duquette. 2–3 – 4 PM production. 4–5 – Hananeko_Studio, prochasson frederic. 6–7 – TTstudio, Sergey Novikov. 8–9 – I Made Pasek, Mark Agnor. 10–11 – Nordroden. 12–13 – Maksim Safaniuk, Mark Agnor. 14–15 – Life In Pixels, Nigel J. Harris. 16–17 – Reese Solomon, Lubo Ivanko. 18–19 – EQRoy, Andy Soloman. 20–21 – Dziurek, View Apart. 22–23 – Jayakri, Littlekidmoment.

CONTENTS

Words that look like this can be found in the glossary on page 24.

AMAZING ADVENTURES!

Transportation is how people and things move around. Some modes of transportation are huge, and others are small. Some have powerful engines, and some are powered by people.

UNDER THE GROUND

Most forms of transportation carry people above the ground. However, millions of people travel under the ground every day. Have you ever ridden in an underground vehicle?

MINING CARTS

A mine is a pit or tunnel in the ground. Mining is when people dig valuable materials, such as metals, out of the ground. Carts were some of the first vehicles used in mines.

Mining carts do not usually carry people. Instead, they hold the mined materials. The carts have wheels that follow a track. They are used to move the mined materials above ground.

DRILL RIGS

Drill rigs are another type of mining machine. Drill rigs are huge, powerful drills attached to vehicles. These rigs can be driven inside the mines to where they are needed.

Drill rigs are mostly used to drill holes and make more tunnels inside mines. Some drill rigs are made for tight spaces. Some are made to drill a hole of a certain size.

LOADERS

Mined material can be very heavy, especially when there is lots of it. Loaders are used for scooping up and carrying mined materials. First, the loaders scoop up the material inside the mine.

Once loaders have scooped up some material, they take it away to clear the area so more mining can happen. Loaders carry the mined material wherever it is needed.

HAUL TRUCKS

Haul trucks are used in large mines. They can move around lots of mined materials. Haul trucks are very strong. They can carry a lot of weight in the truck bed.

Loaders tip mined material into the bed of haul trucks. The haul trucks then drive through the tunnels of the mine. They take the mined materials out of the mine.

UNDERGROUND TRAINS

Underground transportation can be found in many large cities around the world. They often have a network of underground trains. These networks are sometimes called a subway or a metro system.

Subway systems have different routes to take people to different parts of the city. These are called lines.

Subway systems have stations. People take stairs or elevators to get to the underground platforms.

LONDON UNDERGROUND

The London Underground is the oldest metro system in the world. It first opened in 1863. The London Underground is often called "the Tube." In an average year, the Tube is used by over 1 billion passengers.

NEW YORK CITY SUBWAY

The New York City Subway is the largest subway system in the United States. The New York City Subway has over 450 stations.

THE CHANNEL TUNNEL

Some underground trains travel under the seabed. The most famous example of this is the Channel Tunnel. This tunnel is beneath the English Channel, which is the stretch of sea between England and France.

Different kinds of trains travel through the Channel Tunnel. Some of the trains carry passengers. Some carry freight. Some trains even carry people's vehicles across the English Channel.

THE FUTURE OF TRAVEL

The ways people travel under the ground has changed a lot over the years. It is sure to keep changing in the future. Inventors will keep coming up with better vehicles.

Subway systems might continue to get bigger and better. More cities might build them. They might get faster and easier to use. More underground tunnels could connect even more of the world.

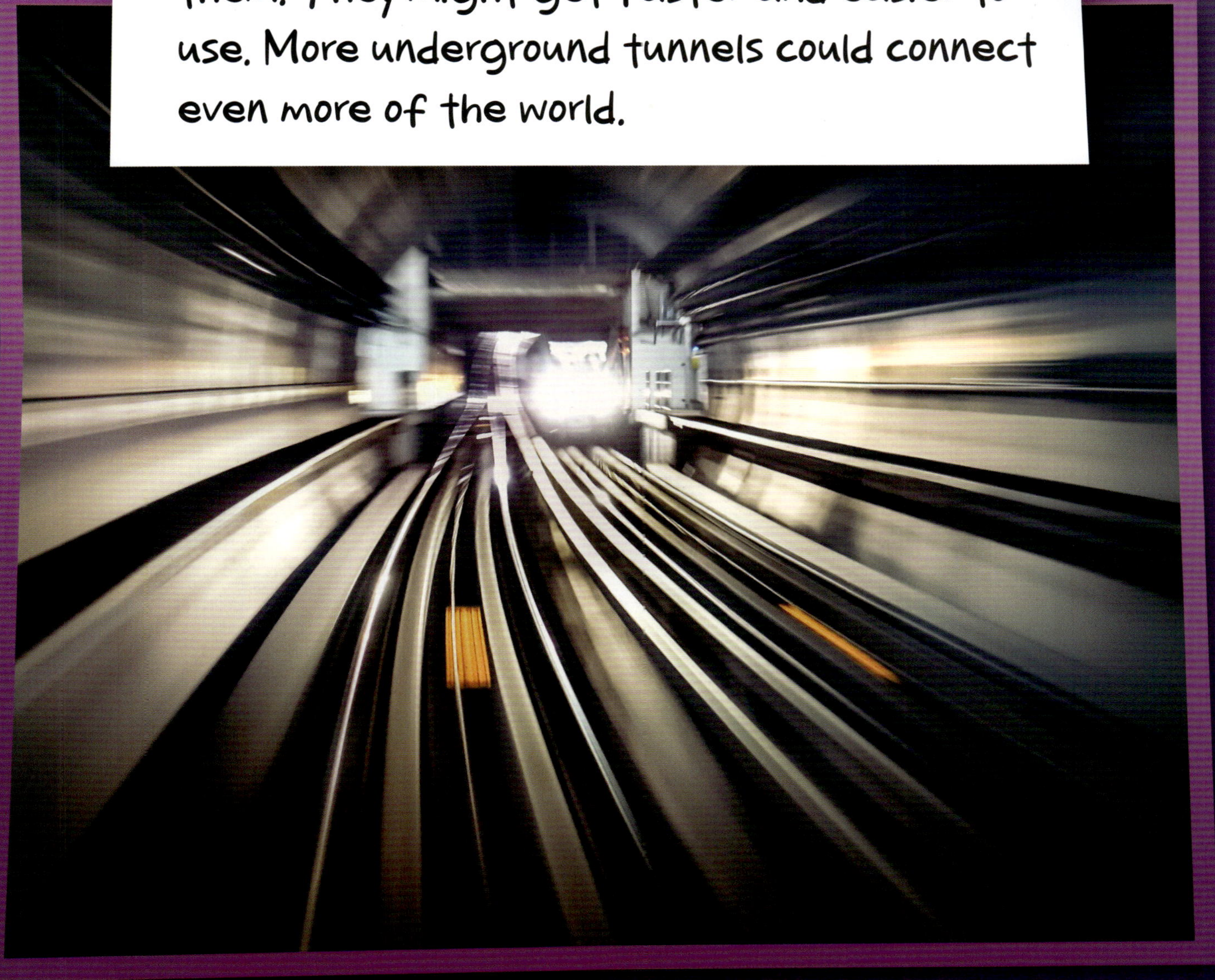

TRANSPORTATION ADVENTURES

There are quite a few ways to use transportation under the ground. Whether you are digging for valuable materials or zooming across a city, the best path might be under the ground!

Going underground might just be the start of your adventure! Have you ever used an underground subway system? What kind of underground vehicles might you want to take a trip on?

GLOSSARY

engines machines that use electricity or fuel to make movement

freight goods that are carried from one place to another

network a group of connected things

platforms where trains stop to let passengers on and off

vehicle a machine that is used to carry people or things

INDEX